THE IMPRESSIONISTS

Henri-Alexis Baatsch

ESSENTIALS

HAZAN

Translated from the French by
Stephen Schwartz

Document de couverture :
Impression. Soleil levant (détail), 1873.

© Éditions Hazan, Paris, 1994

Conception et réalisation :
Anne Anquetil

Photogravure :
Martial Productions, Paris

Achevé d'imprimer en mars 1994
par Milanostampa, Farigliano

Printed in CEE

ISBN 2 85025 368 3
ISSN 1250-5951

THE
IMPRESSIONISTS

SUMMARY

·

Not so long ago, as late as the beginning of the 1950s, locomotives still steamed into the stations. There were no longer many *canotiers* but a few courageous bathers were still willing to hazard a dip in the Seine just downstream from Paris. At Bougival on the Seine, or by the Mane, the riverbank were filled with families out of a Sunday walk. There were still a few real farms in the near suburbs; Italian and German operas were usually still sung in French, without much concern for authenticity be damned, and on race days the racetracks at Longchamps and Auteuil attracted crowds made up of both the elegant in their top hats and the common people in their caps. Like a painting.

After Mass, street singers would belt out popular tunes below the windows of apartment buildings in the middle-class neighbourhoods of nearby Boulogne – on a street that was already known as the "rue Claude-Monet" - until the haggard residents finally threw down a few francs. All over the Ile-de-France one could still find the sort of springtime gathering places that were already on the wane: places like La Grenouillère and the Fournaise restaurant made famous in paintings by Renoir. There being no such thing as *le week-end*, on summer evenings in working-class neighbourhoods people would sit at the window or on the front step to gossip and watch the passers-by. That was their entertainment and their diversion.

That world has long since now truly disappeared. But it lasted for almost 100 years. It was the world of the Impressionists and, as Dame Sei Shonagon put it, writing in 11th-century Japan, "It is now in the past". This notion, of a world both near to us and yet entirely past, is no doubt largely responsible for the mass success of these 19th-century artists, an incontrovertible triumph that has successively conquered countries quite far from the culture and landscape of what were the major centres of Impressionism–the Ile-de-France, Normandy, and Provence–in the last half of the 19th century. All over the world, all those

RENOIR
Mother Antony's Cabaret, 1866.

MANET
Lunch on the Grass, 1863.

DEGAS
The Star or Ballerina on Stage, 1878.

who experienced the industrial invasion of the cities and the end of the peasant era, who partook of the pleasures of city-dwellers, whether bourgeois or working-class, in the course of a 19th century that saw the birth of the "modern" world, all those who in varying degrees lived through that age marked by all manner of upheavals, were happy to once again find themselves in the scenes and the land-scapes depicted by the Impressionists, long before it ever occurred to them to wonder about the pictorial revolution that such work represented.

And it surely was a pictorial revolution. The thirty-odd years through which the Parisian art world passed from the scandal of Manet's *Déjeuner sur l'herbe* [*Picnic on the Grass*] in 1863 until the almost-official recognition of Impressionism constituted by the partial acceptance by the French government in 1894 of the be-quest by Caillebotte (who was himself an Impressionist, a collector and a sup porter of his fellow Impressionists) were certainly exhilar-ating ones. Yet Impressionism, in the popular imagina-tion, was less a new painting technique, a new approach to light, or, as Cézanne would have it, a persistent reflection on the geometrical decomposition of forms, than a choice of "subjects", a reconstitution of a world and an age cap-tured in their truth–without emphasis, posing, or "His tory"–a world approached and apprehended in its sim-plest details.

"One must always be ready to move on for the sake of one's subject. Without baggage. Just a toothbrush and a piece of soap," said Pierre-Auguste Renoir, who wore a beard just to avoid taking a moment out of his morning in order to shave. Such was his summary of the basic ingre-dients of the Impressionist attitude: mobility, the willing-ness to work anywhere and in the most precarious condi-tions, in order to catch–on the wing, as it were–anything worth catching. It was an age of walkers, perpetually moving, with their art supplies ever at the ready. These nomads had provided open-air painting with legitimacy hey then intended to toil to make it illustrious, showing just how much this innovation had revolutionized the conventions of painting and thereby creating the aesthetic of their time.

But what about Degas and his dancers at the Opera? Toulouse-Lautrec and his *Bal du Moulin Rouge* [*Ball at the Moulin-Rouge*]? Caillebotte and his floor carpenters? Why, if an Impressionist is above all one who paints in open air, do we now see *them* as part of the group of Impressionists as well? Perhaps because most of them knew and associated with one another regularly, but also because nowadays we tend to think in terms of the *epoch* rather than in terms of the elements that comprised the daily investigations of each individual. There were fifteen or so members of the group, separated in age by only a few years. They all knew France in the same way, haunted by the joy of life and shaken by the violent political and economic events that the nation experienced during its painful emergence into the industrial age and political stability. These artists were less theoretically sophisticated about their art than they were fervently committed to it, with a naiveté that is often startling. Though not necessarily inclined towards it, some of them knew what it meant to suffer for one's art and could have been aptly described as "tortured artists" (an expression later invented to describe Van Gogh's personal misfortune). Even if they were not "romantics" in the contemporary sense of the word, they had at least one thing in common: enemies, and lots of them.

The "impressionists": the critic Leroy's mocking observations regarding the 1874 exhibiting of Monet's painting *Impression, soleil levant* [*Impression: Sunrise*] hit their target. In fact, the representation of fleeting phenomena, the need for a lighter-coloured palette, the inclination toward open-air work, had by that time already been part of the practices of several of these painters for some ten years. Yet these are the very painters that the "right-thinking" critics of 1874 tried to destroy, and would continue to

TOULOUSE-LAUTREC
At The Ambassadors, Aristide Bruant in His Cabaret, 1892.

NADAR
The Poet Charles Baudelaire, 1855.

do so in the years to come. Indeed, 1874 is the moment when the "group" first began to assert itself, organizing the first of what would officially be eight exhibitions of "independent artists". For the previous ten years, during which a few fervent believers had begun their revolution in painting, disorganizedly confronting the artistic establishment, the "Impressionists" had sufficiently aired their views and put forth their work so that they no longer expected very much from that establishment or its structures. 1874 is thus the decisive year–prepared for in numerous skirmishes–in the birth of an artistic movement as notable as it is beloved because it has the flavour of a newfound artistic and, indeed, human freedom. Frédéric Bazille, one of the earliest of the Impressionists along with Monet and Renoir, had already passed on. He was killed on the front in the lost battle of Beaune-la-Rolande, on 28 November 1870, during the *Année Terrible*[1] of both foreign and civil war in France. Charles Baudelaire, the most clearsighted mind of the age and one of the most ardent defenders of Edouard Manet, had died in 1867. The Republic was finding its way, groping towards stability, adapting to modernity: the great men of art of that time were already in place, producing mature work.

Let us retrace their paths, their undertakings, their wondrous productions.

The Impressionist adventure began in a world of industrialization and urbanization in which the last links to the ageless world of slow, steady evolution had finally been severed. This new atmosphere of freedom permitted the invention and propagation of new technologies with promising futures like photography; it was a world besotted with the steam engines, foundries, and iron that were often ingeniously exploited in the new architecture; a world that saw the daily transformation of distance and darkness that was brought about by the telegraph, gas light, and electricity; this was a world that marvelled at the new-found facility and speed of movement and communication, a world where everyday life had begun to benefit from the inventions of scientists and engineers, those demiurges of time.

Where, in relation to this changing world, was the artistic establishment if a painting of locomotives steaming out of the Saint-Lazare railway station, or a depiction of the winter sky above the roofs and cobblestones of Paris, or a realistic portrayal of a woman drinking absinthe in a café were sufficient to cause a scandal? As the poet Fernand Desnoyers proclaimed in a thundering article from 1855, it was a world that for quite some time had had enough "of underbrush, of the battle of the Cimbri, of the pandemonium of Greek temples, of lyres, of biblical harps, of alhambras, of tubercular oaks, of sonnets, of odes, of daggers and hamadryads in the moonlight." It had had enough but dared not say so. Powerful interests in important social positions and defending an outmoded romantic ethic were fiercely opposed to the adaptation of painting to modernity that was taking place in the permanent workyard that Haussmann's Paris had become.

Courbet's realism had opened a breach within academicism by introducing 19th-century that is, *contemporary*–subjects, but he had not yet altered the work-methods nor had he created a new approach to pictorial *matter*. His *Atelier du Peintre* [*The Artist's Studio*] still demonstrated respect for large formats, for the preparation of the background, for the "manner" of the Ecole, and for the institutional setting, even if, at the same time, it was already an enormous fresco of the varied society of that time. Edouard Manet, obstinate and certain of his own value as he may have been, was at that time still nothing but a solitary investigator.

In France, the Barbizon School of landscape artists and its leader, Corot, took up a similar standpoint to that of the 17th-century Dutch landscape artists. If *grand-papa* Corot, Daubigny, Théodore Rousseau, Diaz de la Peña,

CAILLEBOTTE
The Bridge of Europe, 1877.

MONET
The Bridge of Europe, 1876.

MANET
The Railroad, 1873.

MANET
The Plum, 1878.

even Troyon were already remote from any attempt at
pure and simple studio reconstruction of the atmosphere
that they attempted to capture in the natural light of the
fields and forests, for the most part they also stuck to the
painterly practice of their forerunners, reworking in a uni-
form light the landscapes or country scenes that moved
them, in order to fix those scenes in a kind of miniature
eternity. Millet, for example, was able to memorize and
reconstitute outdoor scenes. These Barbizon artists had an
original regard toward the nature of their time. They
appreciated its manifestations in a way that "academic"
painters, snared within their allegories, or painters of
imaginary historical scenes or "noble" subjects were
unable to do, for they were not only unable to look around
themselves, but completely unwilling to do so as well.

The real history of Impressionism begins in the year
1862-63. Paris was at that time reeling–and the art world
along with it–on its way to becoming "the capital of the
19th century," as the 20th-century German philosopher
and critic Walter Benjamin would aptly put it. Paris was
not only opening to modernity, it *was* modernity itself.
With Haussmann's great reconstruction in the Second
Empire, the capital took on the appearance that, for the
most part, it has today. In the domain of the arts, with the
exception of music, it enjoyed a reputation unrivaled by
any other city. Like the entirety of France at that time, having become imbued over the course of the preceding century with a sense of being an historical model, Paris felt
and believed in its own power. Its institutions and artists
were internationally renowned. The brilliance of Paris-the
art capital, indeed, the cultural capital of Europe–was quite
simply unparalleled. Thus, to have a painting shown at
the grand official Salon, which brought together some two
to three thousand works all of which were more or less
"intelligible" according to their place within the exhibition
was to participate in the established values of a world that
was still quite sure of itself. It also entailed recognition by

he supreme arbiters of artistic value: the directorate of the École des Beaux-Arts and of the Institut de France. Though the imperial regime was an authoritarian one, it had working in its favor not only the popular support from which it derived its strength but the particular intelligence of the sovereign, Napoleon III, and his military prestige abroad. Bismarck may have been lying in wait, but he had not yet moved toward France.

In this world of rapid development, something else had changed that the powers and the existing authorities could not comprehend. The rapid transformation of old ways of life, the proliferation of means of transportation, the relative rapidity of communications, the new relationship to the image (people's image of themselves as well as the new images of other people and things brought about by the dissemination of photography), the new kinds of lighting, metals, industry, chemistry: all of these things served to render obsolete the hieratic, mythologizing, and exotic conception of art of the official dogmas. The official art was henceforth completely out of sync with a society that it towered over without understanding. When it was of high quality, this art had always had its warring deities–sometimes irascible, sometimes good-natured–ike Delacroix and Ingres. And among lesser artists it was neo-gothic versus neo-classical at a time when society as a whole was reeling, confronted with new problems regarding light and artifice and asking itself new questions about its entry on to a path of seemingly infinite discovery. One has to see Thomas Couture's *Les Romains de la décadence* [-*Romans of the Decadence*] at the Musée d'Orsay, or Signol's mythologized triumphs at the church of Saint-Sulpice to witness the extent to which the academic painting of the years 1850-60 had become stilted. It was like a movie industry that produced nothing but *Cleopatra* and *The Ten Commandments*, regurgitating the same historical and mythical tales endlessly, stories that had had the founding virtue of a certain social "order" for the grandparents of

RENOIR
The Boating Party, 1881.

MONET
The Rocky Coast, 1886.

RENOIR
*Portrait of Charles and
Georges Durand-Ruel*, 1882.

the artists themselves. The need for the epic among the little boys who grew up in the shadow of Napoleon had not yet been extinguished.

Developed over the course of a decade, the rupture that we now call "Impressionism" stood before a potentially vast field of action. It was not only a break with tradition carried out by the young, by painters and colourists but also a break in human practices. Simple, everyday life the life of men, women, children, the colours of the seasons and the street, everyday pleasures, walks, the work of ordinary people reclaimed their prerogative. Official bourgeois portraiture had gone out of fashion and had been replaced by the fleeting joys represented in *Déjeuner des Canotiers* [*The Luncheon of the Boating Party*] or the more profound ones of a mother with cradled child. The tormented sky and seas of the romantics gave way to the more realistic–and more readily visible–boiling seas of Belle-Ile or the coast of Normandy. The little villages on the banks of the Oise or the Seine, the tree-lined roads that are so common in France, the somewhat crude but graceful female models, of necessity somewhat easy, always in need of a little money to survive in the big city: all of them would become, on the canvases of Pissarro, Monet, Morisot, Degas, or Renoir the basis of an ever-renewed sense of wonder beneath the light, the brilliance, the mists, the gleam of the hours and days. Some, like Pissarro and Monet, resolutely abandoned the studio mindset, braving without hesitation the worst meteorological conditions to record visual sensations that no painter before them had had the steadfastness to represent *close to*: "Today I painted for part of the day in the steadily falling snow: you would have laughed to see me shrouded entirely in white, my beard covered with icicle 'stalactites.' " (Claude Monet, letter to Gustave Geffroy of 26 February 1895 from Sandviken, Norway).

By 1874, the Impressionist group had been constituted, in the face of a still mostly hostile public. It also had s designated art dealer, Durand-Ruel, who, in the 1880s, attempted to export their work to England and America and continued to have his supporters among the enlightened bourgeoisie. This semi-official status was punctuated by the independent collective shows that he organized until 1886. The beginning was nevertheless difficult, all the more so because the most important politician of the time, Gambetta, did not hesitate to declare (and despite the fact that he was generally favourable towards Impressionism) that "it would be better for the Republic to live with bad painting than to die with great art." And these years were to witness a strange ballet of the participants in these public demonstrations. Pissarro struggled to maintain a certain cohesion in the group but his interest in the younger painters like Gauguin and Seurat also gave rise to violent polemics and temporary ruptures. Degas, the other member of the group's "brain trust", would stubbornly maintain a semblance of collective activity while also serving as the advocate of "intransigence"–in other words abstention from official exhibitions. John Rewald, in his *History of Impressionism*, retraces in detail the whole history of this group, which is in fact a variable constellation of members, with its cafés, its privileged places, its themes, but which in no way seeks to box in any of its members, each of whom fiercely maintained the autonomy of his life, friends, and creative work. The Impressionist milieu introduces us to the whole idea of groups of artists and intellectuals that characterizes modern and even contemporary art. The Impressionists improvised a new and experimental mode of artistic relations: by being open to the immediate subjects suggested by the daily life of their time, they made a definitive break with the ornamental and monumental art that had continued right up until the middle of the century, complete with all its apparatus of the grand studio, the master painter and his students. In other words, they rejected the basic way that painting had functioned since the Renaissance. With the Impressionists,

VAN GOGH
The Bridge in Rain, after Hiroshige, 1887.

MONET
Water-Lilies, 1916-1919.

MONET
Rouen Cathedral,
Sun Effect, 1893.

independently of their particular personalities, art becam
resolutely individual, even individualistic. Like the artist
of the Japanese ukiyo-e, whose representation of life so
adrift on the stream of time they profoundly admired an
recognized as their oriental counterpart, the Impressionist
also pursued their individual paths, even to the point c
specialization. The social conditions of art had changed.
was thus not surprising to find that when renown, an
even fame, finally became accessible to some members c
the group, they moved away from the temporary collectiv
ity of which they were a part in order to pursue their ow
solitary paths.

Some of the later and younger members of the group
having been formed on the job–including Vincent va
Gogh and Gauguin–covered even more quickly the rout
leading from collective approval to rupture and finally t
the solitary quest. Cézanne became a "hermit" in Aix-ei
Provence, seeking his own "truth of painting" in whic
many would come to see the work of a primitive, a new ai
far from the pictorial tradition, but just as far from th
momentary glow of Impressionism that he followed onl
for a time. Monet, the most steadfast as well as the mos
obstinate follower of the line that he had himself definec
would immerse himself in the series of *Haystacks*, of *Pop
lars*, of *Rouen Cathedral*, of views of Westminster and finall
in the *Waterlilies*, a work which is at once painting an
space, world and painting, a work which encompassed hi
life and with which he surrounded himself.

Around 1885, Impressionism had sufficiently estab
lished itself for a rigorous mind like Georges Seurat t
attempt to introduce a real optical science into pictoria
work and, in Neo-Impressionism, to create what has to b
considered the first deliberate theory within art itself.

A few years later the organized activities of the grou
were definitively in the past. The Dreyfus Affair served t
isolate Degas, who responded to the nationalist sirens c
the anti-dreyfusards. The break between the childhoo

iends Zola and Cézanne had already been consummated with the publication of Zola's *L'Œuvre* in which Cézanne recognized himself in the character of Claude Lantier, the failed artist. Van Gogh committed suicide at Auvers because "he was too bored". Gauguin took off for another far off place, the islands of the Pacific, in order to reinvent primitive art with different human values. Monet went travelling, finally settling in Giverny, a setting created for his eye and his conception.

Death had also begun to do its work of dispersion. In 1894, Caillebotte's bequest to the State of his collection of his friends' works, with the stipulation that they be destined for the Louvre, created a final uproar among the traditionalists, simultaneously sealing the importance of the Impressionists within the artistic history–and the history pure and simple–of the previous thirty years. Posterity could only add to the genius of Cézanne and Monet, the virtue of Pissarro and Sisley, while certain others would come to be seen as having had the merit of prefiguring various innovative movements. Which is to say nothing of the lasting astonishment into which future generations will continually be cast by the work of Van Gogh, Gauguin, and even Seurat.

The portrait is now complete. Strangely, however way one looks at them, these moments have become dense, like a late Cézanne, a "real" Cézanne. That was Impressionism, that was the age, and those were the people. They taught us to "see" what most, were satisfied–and are satisfied still–only to look at.

MONET
Water-Lilies, 1916-1919.

MONET
*Rouen Cathedral, The Portal
and the Albane Tower*, 1893.

DAUBIGNY

Stream in the Undergrowth.

In relation to the Impressionists, Daubigny played th role of a precursor, a benevolent precursor. He attached to the movement by the places that inspire him, his taste for painting in open air, and his water land scapes, even though he is clearly closer in age and in h friendships to the Barbizon group of painters.

His solid academic formation – he travelled to Italy the age of nineteen – and his work in the studio of the hi torical painter Delaroche did not prevent him from empha sizing fields and water, impressions of the countryside an the woods that inspired him, from the time of his first su cesses at the Salon, notably the Salon of 1857.

His passion for the play of water led him to mov aboard a combination studio-boat that the women doin their laundry on the banks of the Seine or the Oise used call the *Bottin* or "little box".

Daubigny was also linked to the Impressionists – no ably Pissarro, Cézanne, and all those who frequented th Oise region – by the fact that he made Auvers the hom port from which he launched his various excursions an work sessions on the river. His *Bottin* even found an imit tor in the studio-boat that Monet used at Argenteuil i order to work on the water.

It was with regard to Daubigny's works like *Les Ve danges en Bourgogne* [*The Grape Harvest in Burgundy*], whic was shown at the Salon of 1863, that receptive critics lik Castagnary would for the first time speak of a painting "impressions" and a "painting of the moment". In fa Daubigny was already involved in the great innovation process and was not afraid to state that one "can nev paint clearly enough".

"Daubigny, an ambitious man, a liberal, a free-thinker, practically a materialist!" fervently declared Nieuverkerke, the superintendent of the *beaux-arts* during the Empire. Despite such hostility, Daubigny was on several occasions a member of the jury and was one of the few, along with Corot, to defend the Impressionist generation, which he saw extending his own ideas. During the siege of Paris in 1870, he took refuge in London along with Pissarro and Monet, presenting them to Durand-Ruel, his dealer.

Some of his paintings – *Les Champs au mois de Juin* [*The Fields in the Month of June*] and *La Neige dans la Campagne d'Auvers* [*Snow in the Countryside at Auvers*], for example – express intensely the extent to which the world of his representations was close to that of the great open-air Impressionists. Van Gogh himself was fascinated by his work.

JONGKIND

Holland, Rowing Boats by a Mill, 1868.

Manet considered the "great" Jongkind the father of modern landscape painting. His watercolours were admired as pure marvels by Cézanne and Pissarro. Monet often claimed to be indebted to Jongkind for "the definitive education of my eye".

Jongkind was the first real precursor of the Impressionists. It was in order to evoke Jongkind's *Clairs de lune* [*Moonlight*] and *Vues de la Seine* [*Views of the Seine*] that the critic Castagnary used, for the first time in his critique of the Salon des Refusés in 1863, the notions of "impression" and "effect".

Born in a maritime nation where water is as ever present in painting as it is in life, Jongkind's meeting with the landscape and marine painter Isabey made up his mind to continue his career in Paris. Recognized from the start, to the point of being subsidized until 1853 by the Dutch court, Jongkind lived among the first circle of Impressionists, despite their generational differences. He led a tumultuous life and was led by a combination of debts and an unrestrained bohemianism into several alcoholic depressions so serious that his friends thought him lost on more than one occasion. As a very young Monet put it starkly in a letter to Boudin in 1860: "The only good marine painter we have has died for his art. He is completely crazy. . . . You have a nice role to fill." The support of his friends brought him back several times from the final threshold, especially the love of the woman who was to become his companion, Madame Fesser. Thanks to her efforts, from 1870 he was able to avoid the absolute tragedy toward which he seemed to be headed. Sapped by alcoholism, he finished his days in La Côte-Saint-André, in Isère, painting with watercolours rather than oil paints.

BOUDIN

Seiling Boats at Honfleur, c. 1854-1860.

" To swim in the sky, touch the tender clouds, suspend these masses, in the far off background, in the grey haze, make the azure shine. . ."

The son of a boatswain, Eugène Boudin was familiar with the steamers in Le Havre. He was late to take up painting, pursuing a modest path. But he was a determining influence on the young Monet, whom he encountered in a Le Havre art shop where the latter was showing the fruits of his talent as a caricaturist. Boudin persuaded Monet to try open-airwork with him. By taking this crucial step, the younger man was able to form the core of what was to be his strong personality.

Boudin had been noticed by Isabey and Troyon, who, in order to help him, entrusted him with some preparatory work. In 1859, he met Courbet and Baudelaire, who were visiting Honfleur, and thus earned the esteem of two of the most important personalities of the era. In his *Salon of 1859*, Baudelaire wrote of some pastels that Boudin had showed him that "these quickly and faithfully sketched studies of what is most evanescent and elusive in its form and colour, of waves and clouds, always bear in their margins the date, the time, and the prevailing wind. For example: 8 October, noon, wind from the northwest. . . . If one hides this caption with one's hand, it is still possible to guess the season, the time, and the wind. I am not exaggerating. I have seen it." Even if these studies contain no human forms, Baudelaire's description here is practically the definition of one of the Impressionists' strongest aspirations.

Above all, Boudin's skies provoked the admiration of Courbet, Daubigny, and Corot. Later, Geffroy would class him among the precursors of Impressionism, because, for Boudin, "black does not exist; the air is transparent".

This peaceful man, this "seraph who is familiar with the sky", as Courbet once put it, was a regular visitor to the coasts of Brittany, Normandy and Picardy, and would also travel to Belgium and the Netherlands. Later he would discover Antibes, Juan-les-Pins and Venice.

Though he had never in his life been anything other than a painter, he lacked the material means to embark on a "monumental" work. In 1892, shortly before his death, returning from Normandy, he reminded Monet that together they had once planned "to try their hands at landscape painting in the valley of Rouelles or on the banks of Sainte-Adresse . . . in Trouville and Honfleur with the good and lamented Jongkind."

The Beach at Trouville, 1863.

White Cloud, 1854-1859.

Bathtime, 1864.

Setting Sun and Cliff at Étretat, 1854-1859

PISSARRO

Town's Garden, Pontoise, 1874.

Within the Impressionist "family", Pissarro certainly played the role of the best teacher, as well as that of the good shepherd who guided the strays back to the flock, the better to form a common front against all those who would have liked to see the group break up. His father, a Jewish hardware dealer from Bordeaux who had moved to the Antilles, sent him to study art in Paris where he demonstrated above all a talent for drawing. Returning to the Antilles, he was spotted by the Danish painter Fritz Melbye, who persuaded him to study with him in Venezuela. In 1855, he returned definitively to Paris. During these years of his education, he would also work with Anton Melbye, Fritz's brother, at the Ecole des Beaux-Arts in Paris and on location all over the Ile-de-France. It was during this period that he met Claude Monet: "I met Pissarro in 1858" (letter from Claude Monet in 1925). Having been admitted in 1859 to the Salon and then rejected in 1863, he participated in the Salon des Refusés, the rival salon that was authorized and demanded by the Emperor. In 1861, he first met the "strange Provençal", Cézanne, at the Académie Suisse. As an old man, Cézanne would say: "Pissarro was like a father to me". Manet's *Olympia* in 1865 crystallized the movement. Beginning in 1866, Pissarro would offer his response at the Café Guerbois and later at the Nouvelle Athènes.

Though Pissarro had been overprotected as a youth, he became a convinced anarchist and deliberately chose the most humble and desolate subjects. He moved to Louveciennes. During the Franco-Prussian war in 1870, he fled to London. A number of his paintings served as doormats for the Prussians who set up a butcher's-shop in his house.

Like Monet, who was also a refugee, he became enchanted by the English countryside and discovered the great English painters of the 18th and 19th centuries: Gainsborough, Reynolds, Constable, Turner. After June 1871 he returned to Louveciennes and then to Pontoise in 1872. Cézanne moved with his family to Auvers-sur-Oise in 1872. This was a period of collective exploration with Guillaumin, Gauguin, Piette and others and coincided with the organization of seven of the eight "Impressionist" exhibitions. Pissarro, along with Degas and Monet, was the most active in these exhibitions. Moreover, he was the only one to participate in all of them. Afterwards, the members of the group no longer wanted to be subject to the external constraint of a situation where collective decisions had to be made at every stage. Proof of how difficult it always is to get a group of painters to work together, even when they are close friends!

All his life and despite the hardship and even misery that would mark his career, Pissarro made a point of renewing these friendships and the interior force brought by work undertaken in common and a collective commitment before the public. His consistent and abundant work, focused on effects and outdoor views, never had the prodigious dynamism of, say, Monet, who was engaged in a veritable visionary conquest. But Pissarro was also no doubt closer to the younger generation and was quick to take an interest in Gauguin with whom he found he also shared political views. At another moment he gave in to the enticement of the scientific conceptions of Seurat's pointillism. In short, he was a committed, discreet, and open man.

Lacroix Island, Rouen, Foggy Effect, 1888.

Factory near Pontoise, 1873.

The Wheelbarrow in the Orchard, 1881.

Woman in a Field at Éragny, 1887.

BAZILLE

View of a Village, 1868.

"We marched on Bellegarde through the woods and in beautiful weather, a few explosions audible in the distance, in no hurry. . . . A woodpecker who did not know on which side to fly was fluttering ahead of the battalion for a quarter of an hour. . . ." (Last letter to his parents).

Frédéric Bazille hadn't the time to become well known or create a considerable body of work. He was nevertheless one of the most sympathetic figures of an early Impressionism marked by the fantasies and exorbitant hopes of young people who know that their beliefs will change the world. He passionately participated in discussions, often getting angry when it seemed necessary. He painted his studios on the rue de Furstenberg and the rue de La Condamine. He posed – in who knows how many poses – for Monet's *Déjeuner sur l'herbe* of 1865-66, shared his studio with Renoir, supported Monet during his major material and physical problems, and performed in plays with Sisley. He was in no way in the background and was involved in the same work as the others. And then he disappeared.

His parents were upper-class protestants and friends of the collector Bruyas (the main character of 1854's famous *Bonjour, Monsieur Courbet*) who was himself closely linked to Delacroix and Courbet. Forced by his parents to study medicine, he finally gave it up in 1864, disgusted by the study of cadavers.

He was already a friend of Monet, Renoir, and Sisley who were all, like him, studying with the painter Gleyre through his cousins, the Lejosnes, he made the acquain

ance of Cézanne and, through him, his friends at the
Académie Suisse, Guillaumin and Pissarro. Together, the
group of his friends formed the core of the Impressionist
group, even if it takes more than friendships to form a
group. The other Impressionists, even those as talented as
Manet, never attained this sort of intimacy, or came along
afterwards as part of the outer circle because the group's
commitment had inspired their respect.

Bazille's personal career spans the years from 1863 to
1870. These dates are important: 1863 was the year of
Manet's *Le Bain* [*The Bath*], which has since come to be
known as the *Déjeuner sur l'herbe*, the first brilliant and disturbing revelation of this independent painter; 1870 was the
year of the war, of the "national defence" in which Frédéric
Bazille would be killed, having volunteered for an infantry
regiment, choosing once again to be on the front lines.

Bazille painted his friends, the places familiar to him,
his family, and the countryside of his native Languedoc (*La
Terrasse à Méric* [*The Terrace at Méric*] dates from 1866). He
accompanied Monet on his first wanderings to Fontaine-
bleau and Normandy and demonstrated a love of poetry
and the new music of his time as well as a generous interest in others that lends him the mysterious appeal of committed and enthusiastic souls.

His sixty or so works, along with the great figures in
open air painted by Monet and Renoir before 1870, are tes-
timony to the generous, and still drifting, atmosphere of
the first bursts of what would later become Impressionism.

Landscape at Chailly, 1865.

Aigues-mortes, 1867.

The Wine Harvest, Study, 1868.

The Wine Harvest, Study, 1868.

RENOIR

Dance at the Moulin de la Galette, 1876.

Renoir, or grace itself: the beauty of women, the love of life, the sparkle of lights, scenes of everyday glorified, and the poignant thread of life. Renoir was not an intellectual, although he was not without spirit, alacrity, or cheek. Renoir did not open up new or unexplored pathways in painting and his art contains no message for future generations to decode. His marvellous talent as a colourist disappeared with him, as did his craftsmanship. For he always was an artisan beginning with his education in a Parisian decoration studio, which he undertook to please a father who maintained the values of his native Limoges, i.e., to learn a solid and respectable craft.

As a young man he used to copy on paper fans the works of 18th-century artists. It was at this time that Boucher's *Diane au Bain* [*Diana in the Bath*] first deeply touched him and he would continue to love it all his life. He would never depart from the sort of naive sensuality that led him continually to paint female models or common pleasures, later to sketch his family life which was founded on the values of the people and the land. Degas once said to him about his wife Aline during a meeting of the Tout-Paris: "Your wife looks like a queen among a bunch of circus performers."

To hear his son Jean, the film director, tell it, Renoir's entire politics – and, perhaps, his artistic scheme as well – can be found in his "philosophy of the cork": a cork floats according to the movements of the water that carries it and does not try to direct them. Throughout his entire career he thus unwittingly irritated several of his friends who warranted the name Intransigents more than he did. Degas often defended him, for the simple reason that he was pleasant, not difficult, and attained a happiness while painting that few artists have known. He would sustain this happiness even during his last years at Cagnes-sur-Mer, when illness and rheumatism rendered him unable to rise from his chair and required him to make incredible contortions just to be able to paint.

His unflagging work, the diversity of the subjects that seduced him, and his good-natured outlook made him the most severe observer of those turbulent years. As he himself once put it: "When Pissarro paints a Paris street, he makes it a funeral where I would have made it a wedding party."

La Grenouillère, 1869.

La Grenouillère, 1869.

The Seine at Asnières (La Yole), 1879.

Oarsman at Chatou, 1879.

Madame Monet and Her Son, 1874.

Lunch at the Edge of the River, 1875-1876.

Rocks at l'Estaque, 1882.

Vines at Cagnes, 1908.

View of Cagnes.

DEGAS

Dancing Exam, 1880.

" When the secret of such grace is finally lost . . . men will go to contemplate the Dancers at the Bar, the Green Singer or the Two Ironers to try to imagine everything bitter and exquisite about a 19th century that has been so often maligned while its delicacy its finesse, and even its lyricism and cruel truth have been wilfully ignored."

Degas had distinction, spirit, and was not afraid of the obstacles he might encounter. He was one of the great ones, one of the brusque characters of the time, who could be critical and curt to an absurd extreme. He was an artist; he was possessed.

Unable to paint in the open air due to the frailty of his eyes – especially after his winter tours of guard duty during the siege of Paris – he was a participant in the Impressionist movement more through his commitment as an organizer and his aesthetic choices than through his technique or his "comma-like" brush strokes.

Degas was from an international family: at once French, American, and Italian. As a result, he often travelled in Italy and even visited America. A bachelor, whose private life has remained suffused with secrecy, Edgar de Gas, who signed his works "Degas", was despite such voyages a hardened Parisian. Even if he was less provocative in this domain than was Toulouse-Lautrec, he was a member of the perversely elegant society of the end of the 19th century and was a regular presence at the Opera, the cafés the racetracks and the bordellos.

He was about twenty years old when a first visit to Italy kindled his enthusiasm for the country of Giotto and

Veronese, whom he abundantly copied. His first subjects were classical and inspired by antiquity. From this classical education he would always conserve a taste for collection, smitten as he was by a resolutely Greek ideal of beauty – the beauty of dance, music, and song – that he had the originality to pursue through the realism of his subjects.

He was an astute defender of the Impressionist movement and actively intervened for its acceptance until the day when, isolated by his misanthropy and even more so by his association with the anti-dreyfusards, he decided to take refuge in his own work for as long as his faltering eyes would allow.

At the age of seventy, at a time when his works were already fetching the astronomical sums reserved for the great works of the past, he said to Ernest Rouart: "One must have an elevated idea, not of what one does, but of what one *might* do one day. Without that, it is not even worth the trouble of working."

Racing Horses in a Landscape, 1874.

The Conversation, 1890.

Jockeys in the Rain, 1881.

At the Milliner's, 1882.

Breakfast after the Bath, 1894.

After the Bath, 1888.

SISLEY

"If Claude Monet had not been his contemporary an friend, he would have been the most perfect land scape painter of the end of the last century. Sisle knew it and was unable to avoid letting his bitterne: show," once wrote Murer, a friend, pastry chef, write painter and member of the Impressionist coterie. Sisle was of British citizenship, his family originally from Ken but he was closely tied to the north of France. He wa wealthy early on, before the destitution of his father du ing the Franco-Prussian war; later he would have difficul' earning a sufficient living for himself and his family fro his art alone. Along with Pissarro, he was in the unplea. ant situation of being among the last to achieve recognitio and he died without knowing that all his labour had final borne fruit.

He was a landscape painter, absolutely so, with touch and an approach that were lighter than Pissarro' and a discretion and perseverance that were no doubt pa of his nature. But he was not so "possessed", unlik Monet, to be able to make of landscape painting a veritab. revolution in art. He had a keen interest in literatur Because he was, in this sense, open to worlds other tha that of painters – with their aesthetic discussions and stra egies of exhibition – he kept himself somewhat delibe ately in the shadows of the smoky and noisy café meetin; that did not suit his temperament, even if he was often ab' to charm everyone over dessert "with his clever witticisn and his laughing fits."

Sisley was part of the original Impressionist nucleu having met Renoir, Bazille and Monet in Gleyre's studic where he had signed on in 1862. He was a familiar at th uberge du Cheval-Blanc at Chailly-en-Bière and at the uberge de Marlotte, during the epoch of great begin- ngs. His work follows the path of his various – and often recarious – stays in the Paris area: the Point du Jour, Moret-sur-Loing, Argenteuil, Louveciennes, Port-Marly. . .

Fog, 1874.

Louveciennes, the Heights of Marly, 1873.

Snow in Louveciennes, 1878.

The Seine at Bougival, 1872-1873.

The Seine at Port-Marly, Mound of Sand, 1875.

The Bridge at Moret, 1893.

Moret, the Banks of the Loing, 1892.

MANET

Music at the Tuileries Gardens, 1862.

"In the midst of difficulty, a virile ingenuity from goat's-foot to putty-coloured overcoat, beard and rare blond hair, graying with spirit. In short, mocking a Tortoni, elegant: in the studio, the fury that rushed him confusedly, onto the empty canvas, as if he had neve painted." (Stéphane Mallarmé)

Since the time of Baudelaire, who was his friend there has hardly been a single poet or thinker who has no devoted a long study to Manet's work. For some, he is th true inventor of modern art, the deliberate godfather of Impressionism. For others he is the last figure of the grea classical art whose themes he borrowed and who was onl shocking because the age detested his intellectual freedor as an artist.

Yet he was not an intellectual. He wanted to be painter at all costs. He was of a bourgeois background, staunch republican with an absurdly excessive respect fc conventions, to the point of agreeing to pass off the chil he had out of wedlock as the younger brother of his futur wife. His life was ordered but not without its passions, fc example his passion for Victorine Meurent, the model fc *Olympia* or his more constrained but all-the-more intens ardour for Berthe Morisot, who became his sister-in-law But none of all that predisposed him to play the role c intellectual conscience that he in fact played in the earl Impressionist school.

As early as *La Musique aux Tuileries* [*Music in th Tuilerie Gardens*], with a use of darker tones that astonishe his friends, and despite a longstanding attraction to Span ish subjects that he received from the great masters, h continually sharpened his vision of the contemporar

orld in much the way that Baudelaire called for, moving
eyond all sentimentalism and ideology.

Manet's career is studded with scandals that he did
ot seek to create. On the contrary, he was quite attached
o the idea of official recognition which seemed to him to
o without saying although he would not acquire it until
uite late in his career. He was the instrument of scandal,
uite simply and almost innocently because in every expo-
tion, as Duranty put it in 1874, "through the series of gal-
ries, [Manet's painting] always stands out from the rest."

His first scandal was in 1863 with *Le Bain* which later
ame to be known as *Le Déjeuner sur l'herbe*. An even more
iolent scandal was caused by the *Olympia* in 1865, a "hide-
us", "cadaverous" nude in the eyes of most of the critics of
ie time, the subject of which was taken from Titian and the
reat Spaniards. Those who knew how to interpret painting
eyond the conventions of beauty recognized in *Olympia* the
rmidable autonomy and independence of a painter.

Man of the world as well as of the cafés, Manet
icreased his activity in the last years of his life, when he
ready felt the beginnings of the motor-nerve disorder that,
ıllowing an unsuccessful operation, would eventually kill
ım. Georges Bataille offered the following characterization
f the distance that in fact separated Manet from the Impres-
onists, many of whom were nevertheless his friends:
Manet inscribed a world of research laid down in the sin-
ularity of his subjects. Manet at the origin of Impression-
m? It is possible. But he keeps himself in a depth which is
reign to Impressionism. No one has invested his subject
ith more: if not with more meaning, then with that which,
ryond meaning, is more than meaning."

Young Girl at the Entrance of the Bellevue Garden, 1880.

The House at Rueil, 1882.

The Bench, 1881.

Portrait of the Writer Émile Zola, 1868.

Nana, 1877.

On the Beach, 1863.

Claude Monet in His Studio, 1874.

Argenteuil, 1874.

61

MONET

Water-Lilies, 1917.

Monet, the initiator and patriarch of Impression ism, embodied personally and in his art all the innovative fecundity of the movement that takes its name from his *Impression, soleil levant* of 1872. His late works, especially the Giverny *Waterlilies*, go beyond even the explorations of his mature years. They established him as the inventor of a shimmering, fluid, luminous, and lyri cal vision and as the first to work toward the breaking down of forms.

Monet was also the gifted and somewhat frustrated battler whose solid realism in the conduct of his life com bined with a clever imagination to provide him with the defences that society would not.

He was one of the very first self-made artists, with neither a family to provide real support nor schooling to provide him with a lasting orientation. For us, today, he is a part of all the major struggles that accompanied the birth of modern art. Endowed with the strength that conviction brings, he interests us not because we are touched by the very real difficulties he faced but because of the extreme coherence of his way of proceeding.

It was a long road that lay between, on the one hand the young provincial caricaturist whom Eugène Boudin convinced to take up open-air painting, on location, on the seashore, and in the Normandy countryside – making of the hardworking, stubborn and enchanted Monet the pre mier French landscape artist – and, on the other, the famous and self-assured man of the 1890s who undertook his thematic series of paintings of haystacks and cathe drals. Which is to say nothing of Monet the patriarch Clemenceau's close friend, who retired to a Giverny estate hat he had had specially set up as the place where he would crystallize what had become a great body of work.

Monet's life was too long and too dense to be summarized in a few lines. It would be better to follow it through the places and friends, his family and families, for he was indeed a landscape painter, he was not above painting those close to him, especially in his early years. These paintings are almost like a painted diary. Close to Renoir early on, at least in the diversity of his interests, he invested his artistic approach with the fierce ambition to be recognized as the uncontested master of the new painting. And he succeeded.

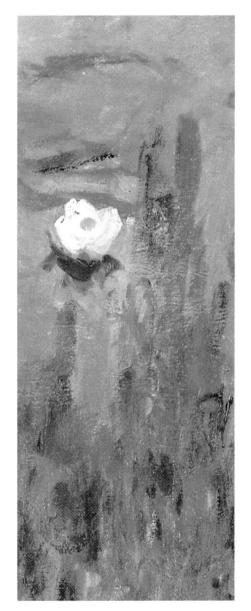

In the Vicinity of Honfleur, 1867.

Sandviken, Norway, Snow Effect, 1895.

The Magpie, 1869.

Snow Effect at Sunset, 1875.

Impression, Rising Sun, 1873.

The Beach at Sainte-Adresse, 1867.

Regattas at Sainte-Adresse, 1867.

The Contarini Palace, 1908.

Venise, le Grand Canal, 1908.

Haystacks, End of the Summer, 1891.

Haystack, Setting Sun, 1891.

Haystack in the Sunshine, 1891.

A Haystack near Giverny, 1886.

MORISOT

Woman and Child on a Balcony, 1872.

She was the daughter of a top functionary and, along with her sister, Edma, studied with Corot, whom she followed and assiduously copied at Ville d'Avray between 1860 and 1862. Berthe Morisot was the most convincing feminine component of Impressionism and one of those young, spiritually powerful women whose high social position allowed her to develop a precious and rare gift. The grave beauty of her features was immortalized in Manet's *Le Balcon* [*The Balcony*], *Le Repos* [*Rest*], *Berthe Morisot au chapeau de plumes* [*Berthe Morisot in Feathered Hat*] and other paintings finished between 1868 and 1870. She was quite close to Manet, to whom she seemed a sort of moral guide. She became the wife of Eugène Manet, Edouard's brother, and was herself an accomplished painter, an inspiration, and a distinguished woman who welcomed as friends not only artists like Degas, Monet and Renoir, but also the poets Stéphane Mallarmé and Henri de Régnier.

Morisot's official career began in 1864, when her *Souvenir des bords de l'Oise* [*Memories of the Banks of the Oise*] and *Vieux chemin à Auvers* [*Old Path at Auvers*] were accepted for the Salon, where she would be accepted every year until she voluntarily withdrew in order to join the exhibitions of the Impressionist group beginning in 1874. At that time, she was more closely linked to what was to be the Impressionists' circle by her common acquaintances than by a specific set of goals. Berthe Morisot would provoke little more than the sort of occasional shameless expressions of contempt or stupid outbursts of hostility that were often the lot of those whom she had chosen as artistic companions and examples. Nor did she frequent

he artists' cafés, for she was obstructed by her status as an
elegant bourgeois woman. Yet she played a part in all of
he exchanges by which an artistic movement is founded
nd sustained.

Outside of Paris and the Oise, her trips to the Brittany
eashore near Fécamp provided her with inspiration. Yet
er talent was of a more intimate sort, one which strove to
lorify the insignificant elements of life, the thread of the
ays that sensibility spins or, as Stéphane Mallarmé put it:
that particularity of a great artist who, even as head of the
ousehold, possessed nothing banal."

Berthe Morisot died of influenza in the winter of
395, leaving her daughter Julie under Mallarmé's tute-
ge, then under that of Renoir and then Degas who would
arry her off to the son of Henri Rouart in 1900. Berthe
ad always been able to organize a life that was welcoming
 artists and poets: this life would carry on in what had
een her home on the rue de Villejust.

It was at that moment that Pissarro wrote to his son,
ucien: "We were all surprised and moved by the disap-
earance of this distinguished woman, of such lovely femi-
ine talent and who honoured our Impressionist group,
nd disappeared as all things must. . . . The public hardly
nows her! It is nothing but speculation that makes names
nd distributes glory. . . ."

The Fable, 1883.

Eugène Manet and His Daughter Julie in the Garden, 1883.

In a Seaside Villa, 1874.

Eugène Manet on the Isle of Wight, 1875.

CASSATT

A delicate painter, with a subtle sense of colour, th
quality of her drawing provoked the unalloye
admiration of Degas. Mary Cassatt played an effec
tive but reserved role in the distribution of her friend
works. Daughter of an American banker, who took her t
visit Europe as early as 1851, she ended up moving t
France after academic studies in America. There she bega
by showing her work in the official Salon of 1872. Dega
whose work she also admired, finally persuaded her i
1877 to join the group, which greeted her more as a co
league than a disciple. She participated in the collectiv
exhibitions of the group, where she presented paintings of
certain intimacy. She also had a passion for colour engrav
ing, dry-point engraving, and pastels, bringing her som
measure of success among connoisseurs like Degas and Pis
sarro, albeit infinitely less among the general public.

She settled in Paris, then, from 1893, in the château c
Mesnil-Théribus in the Oise. Her family was rich enoug
for her to travel – to the United States, Spain, even Egypt.

Her longstanding close and cordial relationship wit
Degas, who willingly accompanied her in Paris and wh
would evoke certain of her features in his paintings, brok
down late in her life at a time when Degas' misanthrop
was growing along with his blindness. She also eventuall
became almost blind and at the age of seventy would hav
to give up painting. It is perhaps in her work that th
attraction felt at the end of the 19th century for the finess
and simplicity exhibited in the art of Japanese engraving i
most clearly expressed.

The Boating Party, 1893.

Summertime, 1916.

Bathing or Two Mothers and Their Children in a Boat, 1910.

Two Children at the Seaside, 1884.

GUILLAUMIN

As a result of a certain immoderation in his colou[r] as well as his influence on Othon Friesz, whom [h]e met in Crozant in 1901, one might see in Guilla[u]min, a discreet but regular member of the Impressioni[st] group, a sort of precursor of Fauvism.

He is nevertheless little-known, no doubt becaus[e] being of humble origins, he was forced to lead a nocturn[al] professional life as a highway maintenance worker. Ear[ly] in the 1870s, Pissarro said of him: "He works at his pain[t]ing during the day and in ditches at night; what courage[!"] Cézanne, Pissarro and Gauguin were among his friend[s,] his advice was welcomed by Van Gogh and Signac, and [he] participated in most of the group's exhibitions. From t[he] time of his days in secondary school at Moulins, he was [a] friend of Murer, himself a painter and writer who, as [a] restorer and collector in Paris, played an important role [in] the distribution of Impressionist works.

Guillaumin's reputation had been made by 1891, [the] year when he had works exhibited at both the Salon d[es] Indépendants and the Cercle des XX in Brussels, when a[n] unexpected lottery gain of 100,000 francs allowed him [to] devote himself entirely to painting. It also gave him t[he] freedom to travel to new landscapes, in the Creuse, in Bri[t]tany, in the South of France, in Holland. Geffroy, the crit[ic] of the time who was closely linked to the Impressionist[s,] remarked that Guillaumin's hallmark "is this viole[nt] imagery and, sometimes, a true richness and a beautif[ul] ferocity".

View of Agay, 1895.

CAILLEBOTTE

Canoes, 1878.

The role that Bazille occasionally played for the first group of Impressionists was taken up in the Impressionists' mature period by Gustave Caillebotte. He was an active patron as well as an excellent painter. At the time of his death in 1894, his bequest to the State of the works of his friends that he had collected provided him with more notoriety than did his very real participation in the movement itself.

After law studies, he was admitted to the Ecole des Beaux-Arts in 1873. In 1876, on Renoir's invitation, he participated in the second Impressionist exhibition where he showed his *Raboteurs de parquet* [*Floor Carpenters*], which is certainly his most famous work as it now hangs in the Musée d'Orsay . The same year, he drafted his first will and testament by which he sought to support by name the future glory of Degas, Monet, Pissarro, Renoir, Cézanne, Sisley and Morisot. In the third Impressionist exhibition, his *Rue de Paris, temps de pluie* [*Paris Street in the Rain*] and *Le Pont de l'Europe* were shown. He participated directly in the organization of the fourth exhibition, showing *La Rue Halévy vue du sixième étage* [*La Rue Halévy seen from the Sixth Floor*], one of the many aerial views of the city that he painted from the balcony of his apartment on the Boulevard Haussmann. He also showed scenes of fishing and boating, leisure activities in which he often participated with Renoir and Monet in Argenteuil and Chatou. One can also see him portrayed in the foreground of Renoir's *Déjeuner des Canotiers*. His more than 300 works in Impressionist style were meticulously composed, and play with perspective and light in a way that makes them a kind of introduction to the work of the Nabis.

Canoes on the Yerres River, 1877.

The Rest, 1877.

Bathers on the Banks of the Yerres, 1878.

CÉZANNE

A Road at Auvers-sur-Oise, 1873-1874.

Was Cézanne a genius? If he was, he was certainl not a genius in the romantic sense, for he devote himself to an ideal discerned early in life whic he pursued and illustrated throughout his entire work: th symbiosis of great erudition and great inspiration.

He was in any case recognized by several of his peer as among the best, even before the Cubists came to recog nize him as the prophet of their own inventions and th inaugurator of the various paths of modern art.

Fierce, timid, quick-tempered to the point of occa sionally stamping on his own paintings, deliberately pro vocative in his attitudes and dress – "I will not shake you hand, Monsieur Manet, for I have not washed for tw weeks!" – he remained all his life the "strange character that Pissarro first met in the 1860s.

He was the son of a well-to-do hatter who became banker in Aix-en-Provence and who, despite numerou disputes, provided Cézanne with sufficient income to liv solely as an artist. Cézanne would move many times in th course of his life, but within a rather limited area. It was a if he could not and would not break with Provence, wher his first and most lasting friendships had been formed likewise his love of freedom and the beauty of nature. A someone whose favourite smell was that of the fields, h never felt at ease in Paris, though he stayed there often.

Zola, a fellow student and friend from secondar school who at one time wanted to promote him and hel him to establish himself, would later break from him, mos notably in *L'Œuvre* which tragically concluded fror Cézanne's attitude that he was a failed artist. Zola n doubt could not understand that a painter's obsessio

ould be as important and obstinate in its field as was
,ola's in the field of literary realism.

Cézanne made painting denser at a time when the
ther Impressionists were dissipating it into so many
moments". Above all, he wanted to make of his art and of
he art of his time "something solid and durable like the art
n museums".

The master of Mount Sainte-Victoire, the progenitor
f a new art, as he has been called, left to posterity in his
tters several keys to the interpretation of his work. For-
nulated in simple language, these letters tell, without
xplaining, what it was that possessed him in the act of
ainting, in any act of painting:

"I owe you the truth in painting and I will give it to
ou . . . For progress to be made, there is only nature; the
ye becomes educated upon contact with it. It becomes
oncentric through looking and working."

Through this will to escape contingency, Cézanne,
ader of Virgil, put forth the only sacred words of his
me.

Chestnut Trees and Farm at Jas de Bouffan, 1885-1887.

The Sea at l'Estaque, 1884.

Winding Road in Provence, 1868.

The Red Rock, 1890.

The Sainte-Victoire Mountain Seen from Bibémus, 1887.

Le Château-Noir, 1900-1904.

The Annecy Lake, 1896.

TOULOUSE-LAUTREC

At the Bar, 1887.

Toulouse-Lautrec was the son of an aristocratic family from the South of France, and of a somewhat extravagant father of whom he would say that "wherever my father is, one is sure of not being the most remarkable person". Toulouse-Lautrec had fragile bones and it was no doubt because of two unfortunate fractures, in 1878 and 1879, that his growth stopped and that the pictorial development of his gift as a keen observer of men grew. Freed by his aristocratic origins from certain ordinary social prejudices and marginalized by his small size and difficult gait – which necessitated the use of a cane – he was not afraid to set up shop in cabarets and bordellos and, while keeping up appearances, to fall into an alcoholic binge that he himself would refer to as a "moral suicide".

"I belong to no school. I work on my own. I admire Degas and Forain" (1891). In 1884, Toulouse-Lautrec began his work as the illustrator of life in the cafés and cabarets of Montmartre: Le Rat-Mort, L'Elysée-Montmartre, Le Chat-Noir, later Le Mirliton, Le Moulin de la Galette and finally Le Moulin-Rouge where he had a reserved table every night. His posters and drawings extol the celebrities of the day like La Goulue, Valentin le Désossé, Grille d'Egout, later the clown Chocolat and the dancer Jane Avril. Though he was killing himself with alcohol in the course of his dissolute nocturnal life, he also managed to travel, visiting England, Crotoy, Spain, and sailing in the Bassin d'Arcachon. On both sides of this double life, he showed a remarkable gift as an observer of social life, of movement, of human beings, and of animals. By pushing these themes – which were similar to those of Degas – to their expressive extreme, he became one with his world nd his age, with what was unique at that time about Paris nd Montmartre. So much so that even though he arrived n the scene too late to become closely involved with the npressionists, he remains for us today a kindred spirit ho, with his particular genius, provided another aspect their efforts.

The First Communion Day, 1888.

The Old Horse of the Omnibus Company, 1888.

At the New Circus, the Clowness with Five Shirt Fronts, 1892.

The Clowness, 1895.

GAUGUIN

Bunch of Flowers, 1897.

"The unbridled wild wolf", as Degas called him charged through life like a combative rebel, constantly called to go further in space and time beyond a movement that he judged insufficiently ambitious as it was able to answer only in the idiom of the French spirit of the age questions that he posed in the idiom of humanity itself.

Gauguin's life, was filled with arduous work, militan commitments at the expense of his friends, chimerica dreaming, fleeting happiness, discoveries always mad *elsewhere*, the painful and glorious satisfaction of a ma who knows that he has defined his own freedom, that he i animated by a spirit that cannot be taken from him.

He thought himself to be wild and primitive eve when he worked for brokerage houses and enjoyed all th privileges that easy money brings with it. He was sti enterprising, a speculator even, when he felt the need t take off for far-off places, as far as the most remote island of the Pacific. Certain family ties and the premature deat of his father during the crossing of the Atlantic resulted i his passing his early childhood in Lima, Peru. Later, at th time of the construction of the canal, he sought to make fortune in Panama. He considered moving to Madagasca before finally opting for the even greater cultural isolatio of Tahiti, then the Marquesas Islands. It was as if life fa from the European world had always haunted him.

His teacher, Arosa, got him a job as a broker an introduced him to the world of art. It was also throug Arosa that he met Mette Gad, a young Danish woman wh became his wife in 1873, at a time when he was alread working steadily on his painting. They would break up i

885, around the time he took up painting full time and ecided that he could not adapt to Denmark.

He paid his first visit to Brittany, to Pont-Aven, in 886, went to Panama and then Martinique in 1887, and ecame friends with Emile Bernard, Daniel de Monfreid, nd the Van Gogh brothers. Back in Pont-Aven, then in rles at the invitation of Vincent – whom he brutally abanoned during the latter's attack of insanity that resulted in is cutting off a piece of his earlobe – then in Pouldu, Gauuin elaborated his new and colourful style.

The years 1888-1890, a time when he was hampered by naterial difficulties, were spent preparing his departure.The scination engendered in him by what he knew of Khmer rt, the art of India and Java and of Utamaro, only served to ncrease his yearning. This individualistic turn in his rogress as a recognized great painter – let alone as one who roclaimed himself as such – did not fail to provoke ridicule nd enmity among those who, like Pissarro, were his first upporters. But, as the "leader" of the symbolist school, he as sufficiently skilled to arrange for the collective support f the artists and poets he needed for his departure.

He arrived in Tahiti in the spring of 1891 and spent ie next two years there. The flop that ensued upon his rst return to France led him definitively back to Oceania,) Tahiti in 1895 then to Hiva-Hoa in the Marquesas in)01, where he died of exhaustion in 1903.

The wild years at the end of his life were at once the appiest and the most difficult. Having left a world that e did not love, he finally became a being who desired ily *to be* :" Where do we come from? Who are we? /here are we going?"

Brittany Landscape, the Mill, 1894.

Brittany Landscape, 1888.

Hello, Mister Gauguin, 1889.

*Vase of Flowers
on a Window Sill*, 1881.

Tahitian Women Bathing, 1892.

When Will You Marry? 1892.

VAN GOGH

The Harvest, 1888.

« Carded by Van Gogh's nail,
   the countryside shows its hostile flesh. . . »

Antonin Artaud knew what he was talking about having undergone a similar experience of madness and psychiatric internment. His long poem *Van Gogh, le suicidé de la société* [*Van Gogh, Society's Suicide Victim*], written in 1947 in a state of intense emotion brought on by a visit to the Orangerie Museum gives up all pretence of being an external critique. Van Gogh did not prefigure anything, he was both the object and the subject of his painting. His cypress trees, his sunflowers, his crows, his room, even his self-portraits have no place within the history of the human gaze. They create a form of seeing. The anecdote at their origin disappears, the preoccupation with expressing an outside spectacle as well; what is left is a presence towards the world and its visual formulation. And because the presence of the world was too strong for him, he had to disappear.

Others would later take up Van Gogh's pictorial technique, thereby creating Fauvism, just as he, in his lucid constructions, had been able to strip the visual education that he received from the Impressionists of all its theatrical qualities. "I am risking my life in my work, and my reason has halfway succumbed to it." On a Sunday evening, 27 July 1890, he lingered on at the inn at Auvers-sur-Oise after having shot himself in the area of the heart: "I was too bored; I killed myself." He died on the 29th, in the arms of Theo, his brother, friend, confident, support within society and companion in adolescent wanderings.

The two Van Goghs were inseparable: one created the

dazzling, relentless body of work, interrupted by a madness that was terrible for him and disturbing for others. The other, Theo, worked to assure that this work left its mark on an art milieu that, at the time, was self-satisfied and restive, having barely begun to perceive the high quality of the work of other Impressionists and unable to understand the breach opened by Vincent. For his was a visual art meant to apprehend earth and space.

As the son of a pastor, Van Gogh was himself possessed by a need to preach, help, and teach the destitute. Through his job at the Galerie Goupil at the tender age of 16, he gained access to the world of art and museums. He quickly became "homesick for the homeland that exists in paintings". This violent and consuming aspiration would become more tangible after 1880, although he had already been drawing for quite some time. His correspondence with Theo documents in detail the astounding decade that followed: a decade overflowing with work, marked by psychic crises aggravated by alcohol and a desperately chaotic love life; a decade which included not only his discovery of the city of Arles to which he summoned Gauguin, but also the catastrophe of Christmas 1889 in which he cut off part of his earlobe to offer it to a prostitute; a decade that brought about his internment and despair. But Van Gogh's life as it can be read in his work, escapes from the art – especially the painting – of his time in order to become fundamental human experience. It is only as such that we can understand it.

"Van Gogh in the end wanted to get back to the infinite toward which, he claimed, one embarks as one would embark on a train headed for a star" (Antonin Artaud).

Olive Trees, Orange Sky, 1889.

Olive Trees, 1889.

Starry Night, 1889.

Starry Night, 1888.

Café at Night, 1888.

The Ballroom, 1888.

The Terrace of the Café on the Forum Square, 1888.

Vineyard at Auvers, 1890.

The Plain near Auvers, 1890.

The Flower Garden, Arles, 1888.

The Sower, 1888.

SEURAT

*A Sunday Afternoon
at the Grande Jatte*, 1884-1885.

All those who knew him, beginning with Arsèr Alexandre, noticed Seurat's seriousness, "never le ting himself lapse into fantasy". At the age (twenty-eight, he wanted to prove that "his theory was no only interesting for open-air subjects, but was also appl cable to large figures painted indoors; it was then that h painted his *Poseuses*." His theory was the theory of pointi lism, of which, through rigour and perseverance, h became the purest and most ephemeral representativ even if he succeeded in persuading others, like his frien Paul Signac and, for a time, Camille Pissarro, to follo him. Pointillism, or Neo-Impressionism, which Signac, i his rigorous and orderly presentation in *D'Eugène Delacro au néo-Impressionisme* [*From Eugène Delacroix to Neo-Impre. sionism*], referred to even more aptly as "the division" though it shares Impressionism's palette, is distinguishe from it by its "optical mixture, the separation of its stroke and its methodical and scientific technique."

Seurat was fascinated early on by the writings (David Sutter on optical beauty, the research of Charle Blanc, and Chevreul's *La Loi du contraste simultané des co leurs* [*The Law of the Simultaneous Contrast of Colours* From them he extracted the most extreme applications fc painting.

In his short life, which was brutally interrupted i March 1891 by a fatal throat infection contracted hangin paintings for the Salon des Indépendants, Seurat worked fc almost a year on each of his exceedingly complex painting This labour allowed him to determine, without speculatio the almost objective price of his work *Les Poseuses* [*The Mo els*]: "I count as expenses seven francs per day for one year.

a Baignade [*Bathers*], the *Grande Jatte*, *Les Poseuses*, *Le Bec du* *loc*, *La Mer à Grandcamp* [*The Sea at Grandcamp*], *Le Chahut*, *e Cirque* [*The Circus*]: with many seashores and the effects f water and forests, Seurat's subject matter is similar to hat of Impressionism. But, in fact, his intention was ntirely different and he claimed, "I could just as well have ainted, in another sort of harmony, the battles of the loraces and the Curiaces. . . ." It was as though he chose aturalist subjects as a kind of tease, the most important art of his work being to apply his method to everything hat Impressionism had overinvested with the *intuition* hat was its greatest strength but which he saw as some- hing like a weakness.

Initially attracted by Courbet, Millet, the Barbizon ainters, realistic scenes (*Le Faucheur* [*The Reaper*], *Les* *aneuses* [*The Haymakers*], *Le Casseur de pierres* [*The Rock-* *reaker*]) and the countryside of the Ile-de-France, he com- leted his break with the Impressionist spirit when he egan to approach the same open-air themes and Parisian musements as a pure and non-anecdotal work on light self, notably in *Un dimanche après-midi à la Grande-Jatte* *Sunday Afternoon on the Island of La Grande-Jatte*], which he ompleted in March 1885. From that time on he was con- idered the leader of a school and, despite the upheaval reated by his attitude and new requirements, each of his ubsequent works was welcomed as a demonstration by he master. Yet he was a contested master, one of the three r four *fin de siècle* inventors of a modernity that would nly be confirmed and see its rhythms adopted some ten r twenty years later.

The Seine at Courbevoie, 1885.

Corner of the Pool, Honfleur, 1886.

LIST OF ILLUSTRATIONS

24. Boudin, *La Plage de Trouville*
(The Beach at Trouville), 1863, oil on
canvas, 43 x 72 cm. Private Collection.

Nuage blanc (White Cloud), 1854-1859,
pastel, 15 x 22 cm. Musée Eugène-Boudin,
Honfleur.

25. Boudin, *L'Heure du bain* (Bathtime),
1864, oil on canvas, 41 x 65 cm.
Private Collection.

Couchant et falaise (Étretat) (Setting Sun
and Cliff at Étretat), 1854-1859, pastel.
Musée Eugène-Boudin, Honfleur.

26-27. Pissarro, *Le Jardin de la ville,
Pontoise* (Town's Garden, Pontoise), 1874,
oil on canvas, 60 x 73 cm.
Private Collection.

28. Pissarro, *L'Île Lacroix, Rouen.
Effet de brouillard* (Lacroix Island, Rouen,
Foggy Effect), 1888, oil on canvas, 44
x 55 cm. Philadelphia Museum of Art.

Usine près de Pontoise (Factory near
Pontoise), 1873, oil on canvas, 47.7x 55.9
cm. Museum of Fine Arts, Springfield.

29. Pissarro, *La Brouette, verger*
(The Wheelbarrow in the Orchard),
1881, oil on canvas, 54 x 65 cm.
Musée d'Orsay, Paris.

Femme dans un clos à Éragny (Woman in
a Field at Éragny), 1887, oil on canvas, 54
x 65 cm. Musée d'Orsay, Paris.

30-31. Bazille, *Vue de village* (View of
a Village), 1868, oil on canvas, 130 x 89 cm.
Musée Fabre, Montpellier.

32. Bazille, *Paysage à Chailly* (Landscape at
Chailly), 1865, oil on canvas, 82 x 105 cm.
The Art Institute of Chicago.

Aigues-Mortes, 1867, oil on canvas, 0.46
x 0.55 cm. Musée Fabre, Montpellier.

33. Bazille, *Vendange (étude)* (The Wine
Harvest, Study), 1868, oil on canvas,
38 x 46 cm. Musée Fabre, Montpellier.

Vendange (étude) (The Wine Harvest,
Study), 1868, oil on canvas, 38 x 46 cm.
Musée Fabre, Montpellier.

34-35. Renoir, *Le Bal du Moulin de la Galette*
(Dance at the Moulin de la Galette),
1876, oil on canvas, 131 x 175 cm.
Musée d'Orsay, Paris.

36. Renoir, *La Grenouillère*, 1869,
oil on canvas, 59 x 60 cm.
Pushkin Museum, Moscow.

La Grenouillère, 1869, oil on canvas, 66
x 86 cm. Nationalmuseum, Stockholm.

37. Renoir, *La Seine à Asnières (La Yole)*
(The Seine at Asnières [La Yole]), 1879,
oil on canvas, 71 x 92 cm.
National Gallery, London.

Les Rameurs à Chatou (Oarsman at Chatou),
1879, oil on canvas, 81 x 100 cm. National
Gallery of Art, Washington.

38. Renoir, *Madame Monet et son fils*
(Madame Monet and Her Son), 1874,
oil on canvas, 51 x 68 cm. National Gallery
of Art, Washington.

Le Déjeuner au bord de la rivière (Lunch
at the Edge of the River), 1875-1876, oil
on canvas, 55.1 x 65.9 cm. The Art Institute
of Chicago.

39. Renoir, *Rochers à l'Estaque* (Rocks at
l'Estaque), 1882, oil on canvas, 66 x 80 cm.
Museum of Fine Arts, Boston.

Les Vignes à Cagnes (Vines at Cagnes), 1908, oil on canvas, 46 x 55 cm. The Brooklyn Museum, New York.

40-41. Renoir, *Vue de Cagnes* (View of Cagnes), oil on canvas. Saarland Museum, Sarrebrück.

42-43. Degas, *Examen de danse* (Dancing Exam), 1880, pastel and charcoal on vellum, 63.4 x 48.2 cm. The Denver Art Museum.

44. Degas, *Chevaux de course devant un paysage* (Racing Horses in a Landscape), 1874, pastel, 48.9 x 62.8 cm. Thyssen-Bornemisza Collection, Madrid.

La Conversation (The Conversation), 1890, pastel, 54 x 66 cm. Private Collection.

45. Degas, *Jockeys sous la pluie* (Jockeys in the Rain), 1881, pastel, 47 x 65 cm. Art Gallery and Museum, Glasgow.

Chez la modiste (At the Milliner's), 1882, pastel, 79.9 x 84.8 cm. Thyssen-Bornemisza Collection, Glasgow.

46. Degas, *Après le bain* (After the Bath), 1888-1892, pastel, 104 x 99 cm. National Gallery, London.

47. *Le Petit Déjeuner après le bain* (Breakfast after the Bath), 1894, pastel, 99.5 x 59 cm. Tel Aviv Museum.

48-49. Sisley, *Rue de la Princesse, Louveciennes* (Street of the Princess at Louveciennes), 1873, oil on canvas, 55 x 47 cm. Private Collection, Dallas.

50. Sisley, *La Neige à Louveciennes* (Snow in Louveciennes), 1878, oil on canvas, 61 x 50.5 cm. Musée d'Orsay, Paris.

51. Sisley, *Le Brouillard* (Fog), 1874, oil on canvas, 50.5 x 65 cm. Musée d'Orsay, Paris.

Louveciennes, hauteurs de Marly (Louveciennes, the Heights of Marly), 1873, oil on canvas, 38 x 46.5 cm. Musée d'Orsay, Paris.

52. Sisley, *La Seine à Bougival* (The Seine at Bougival), 1872-1873, oil on canvas. Musée d'Orsay, Paris.

La Seine à Port-Marly, tas de sable (The Seine at Port-Marly, Mound of Sand), 1875, oil on canvas, 54.5 x 73.7 cm. The Art Institute of Chicago.

53. Sisley, *Le Pont de Moret* (The Bridge at Moret), 1893, oil on canvas, 73.5 x 92.5 cm. Musée d'Orsay, Paris.

Moret, bords du Loing (Moret, the Banks of the Loing), 1892, oil on canvas, 60.5 x 73 cm. Musée d'Orsay, Paris.

54-55. Manet, *La Musique aux Tuileries* (Music in the Tuileries Gardens), 1862, oil on canvas, 76 x 118 cm. National Gallery, London.

56. Manet, *Jeune Fille au seuil du jardin de Bellevue* (Young Girl at the Entrance of the Bellevue Garden), 1880, oil on canvas, 151 x 115 cm. Bührle Collection, Zurich.

57. Manet, *La Maison de Rueil* (The House at Rueil), 1882, oil on canvas, 78 x 92 cm. National Museum of Prussia, Berlin.

Le Banc (The Bench), 1881, oil on canvas, 65.1 x 81.2 cm. Private Collection.

58. Manet, *Portrait d'Émile Zola* (Portrait of the Writer Émile Zola), 1868, oil on canvas, 146.5 x 114 cm. Musée d'Orsay, Paris.

59. Manet, *Nana*, 1877, oil on canvas, 154 x 115 cm. Kunsthalle, Hamburg.

60. Manet, *Argenteuil*, 1874, oil on canvas, 149 x 115 cm. Musée des Beaux-Arts, Tournai.

61. *Sur la plage* (On the Beach), 1863, oil on canvas, 59.6 x 73.2 cm. Musée d'Orsay, Paris.

Claude Monet dans son atelier (Claude Monet in His Studio), 1874, oil on canvas, 82.4 x 104 cm. Neue Pinakothek, Munich.

62-63. Monet, *Nymphéas* (Water-Lilies), 1917, oil on canvas, 150 x 200 cm. Neue Pinakothek, Munich.

64. Monet, *Environs de Honfleur* (In the Vicinity of Honfleur), 1867, oil on canvas, 81 x 100 cm. Musée d'Orsay, Paris.

Sandviken, Norvège, effet de neige (Sandviken, Norway, Snow Effect), 1895, oil on canvas, 73 x 92 cm. Private Collection.

65. Monet, *La Pie* (The Magpie), 1869, oil on canvas, 89 x 130 cm. Musée d'Orsay, Paris.

Effet de neige au soleil couchant (Snow Effect at Sunset), 1875, oil on canvas, 89 x 130 cm. Musée Marmottan, Paris.

66-67. *Impression, soleil levant* (Impression, Rising Sun), 1873, oil on canvas, 48 x 63 cm. Musée Marmottan, Paris.

68. Monet, *La Plage à Sainte-Adresse* (The Beach at Sainte-Adresse), 1867, oil on canvas, 75.8 x 102.7 cm. The Art Institute of Chicago.

Les Régates à Sainte-Adresse (Regattas at Sainte-Adresse), 1867, oil on canvas, 75 x 101 cm. The Metropolitan Museum of Art, New York.

69. Monet, *Le Palais Contarini* (The Contarini Palace), 1908, oil on canvas, 73 x 92 cm. Private Collection.

Venise, le Grand Canal (Venice, le Grand Canal), 1908, oil on canvas, 73 x 92cm. Museum of Fine Arts, Boston.

70. Monet, *Les Meules, fin de l'été* (Haystacks, End of the Summer), 1891, oil on canvas, 60.5 x 100.5 cm. Musée d'Orsay, Paris.

Meule, soleil couchant (Haystack, Setting Sun), 1891, oil on canvas, 73 x 92 cm. Museum of Fine Arts, Boston.

71. Monet, *Meule au soleil* (Haystack in the Sunshine), 1891, oil on canvas, 60 x 100 cm. Kunsthaus, Zurich.

Une Meule près de Giverny (A Haystack near Giverny), 1886, oil on canvas, 61 x 81 cm. Saint-Petersburg, Hermitage Museum.

72-73. Morisot, *Femme et enfant au balcon* (Woman and Child on a Balcony), 1872, oil on canvas, 60 x 50 cm. Private Collection.

74. Morisot, *La Fable* (The Fable), 1883, oil on canvas, 65 x 81 cm. Private Collection.

Eugène Manet et sa fille au jardin (Eugène Manet and His Daughter Julie in the Garden), 1883, oil on canvas, 60 x 73.5 cm. Private Collection.

75. Morisot, *Dans une villa au bord de la mer* (In a Seaside Villa), 1875, oil on canvas. Norton Simon Foundation, Pasadena.

Eugène Manet à l'île de Wight (Eugène Manet on the Isle of Wight), 1875, oil on canvas, 38 x 46 cm. Private Collection.

76-77. Cassatt, *La Partie de bateau* (The Boating Party), 1893, oil on canvas, 90.5 x 117 cm. National Gallery of Art, Washington.

78. Morisot, *Deux Enfants au bord de la mer* (Two Children at the Seaside), 1884, oil on canvas, 97 x 74 cm. National Gallery of Art, Washington.

79. Morisot, *L'Été* (Summertime), 1880, oil on canvas, 73.5 x 99 cm. Armand Hammer Collection, Los Angeles.

Le Bain ou deux mères et leurs enfants en bateau (Bathing or Two Mothers and Their Children in a Boat), oil on canvas, 97.5 x 130 cm. Musée du Petit Palais, Paris.

80-81. Guillaumin, *Vue d'Agay* (View of Agay), 1895, oil on canvas, 73 x 92 cm. Musée d'Orsay, Paris.

82-83. Caillebotte, *Périssoires* (Canoes), 1878, oil on canvas, 157 x 113 cm. Musée des Beaux-Arts, Rennes.

84. Caillebotte, *Périssoires sur l'Yerres* (Canoes on the Yerres River), 1877, oil on canvas, 103 x 156 cm. Milwaukee Art Center.

La Sieste (The Rest), 1877, pastel, 36 x 53 cm. Wadsworth Atheneum, Hartford.

85. Caillebotte, *Baigneurs, bords de l'Yerres* (Bathers on the Banks of the Yerres), 1878, oil on canvas, 117 x 89 cm. Private Collection.

86-87. Cézanne, *Route à Auvers-sur-Oise* (A Road at Auvers-sur-Oise), 1873-1874, oil on canvas, 55 x 46 cm. National Gallery of Canada, Ottawa.

88. Cézanne, *Route tournante en Provence* (Winding Road in Provence), 1868, oil on canvas, 91 x 71 cm. Museum of Fine Arts, Montréal.

89. Cézanne, *Marronniers et ferme au Jas de Bouffan* (Chestnut Trees and Farm at Jas de Bouffan), 1885-1887, oil on canvas, 65 x 81 cm. D.T. Schiff Collection, New York.

La Mer à l'Estaque (The Sea at l'Estaque), 1884, oil on canvas, 73 x 92 cm. Picasso Collection, Paris.

90. Cézanne, *Le Rocher rouge* (The Red Rock), 1890, oil on canvas, 91 x 66 cm. Musée de l'Orangerie, Paris.

91. Cézanne, *La Montagne Sainte-Victoire vue de Bibémus* (The Sainte-Victoire Mountain Seen from Bibémus), 1887, oil on canvas, 65 x 81 cm. Baltimore Museum of Art.

Le Château-Noir, 1900-1904, oil on canvas, 73.7 x 96.6 cm. National Gallery of Art, Washington.

92-93. Cézanne, *Le Lac d'Annecy* (The Annecy Lake), 1896, oil on canvas, 65 x 81.3 cm. Home Houses Trustees, London.

94-95. Toulouse-Lautrec, *Au bar* (At the Bar), 1887, oil on canvas, 55 x 42 cm. Mellon Collection, Upperville.

96. Toulouse-Lautrec, *Le Jour de la première communion* (The First Communion Day), 1888, charcoal and oil on board, 65 x 37 cm. Musée des Augustins, Toulouse.

97. Toulouse-Lautrec, *Le Côtier de la compagnie des omnibus* (The Old Horse of the Omnibus Company), 1888, oil on board, 80 x 50 cm. Jacques Dubourg Collection, Paris.

98. Toulouse-Lautrec, *Au nouveau cirque, la clownesse aux cinq plastrons* (At the New Circus, the Clowness with Five Shirt Fronts), 1892, charcoal and watercolour on paper, 59.5 x 40.5 cm. Philadelphia Museum of Art.

99. Toulouse-Lautrec, *La Clownesse* (The Clowness), 1895, oil on board, 57 x 42 cm. Musée d'Orsay, Paris.

100-101. Gauguin, *Bouquet de fleurs* (Bunch of Flowers), 1897, oil on canvas, 57 x 42 cm. Musée Marmottan, Paris.

102. Gauguin, *Bonjour, monsieur Gauguin* (Hello, Mister Gauguin), 1889, oil on canvas, 113 x 92 cm. Narodni Gallery, Prague.

103. Gauguin, *Paysage de Bretagne, le moulin* (Brittany Landscape, the Mill), 1894, oil on canvas, 73 x 92 cm. Musée d'Orsay, Paris.

Paysage breton (Brittany Landscape), 1888, oil on canvas, 73 x 93 cm. Lucille Ellis Simon Collection, Los Angeles.

104-105. Gauguin, *Vase de fleurs à la fenêtre* (Vase of Flowers on a Window Sill), 1881, oil on canvas, 19 x 27 cm. Musée des Beaux-Arts, Rennes.

106. Gauguin, *Femmes tahitiennes se baignant* (Tahitian Women Bathing), 1892, oil on canvas, 110 x 89 cm. Robert E. Lehmann Collection, New York.

107. Gauguin, *Quand te maries-tu?* (When Will You Marry?), 1892, oil on canvas, 101.1 x 77.5 cm. Kunstmuseum, Basel.

108-109. Van Gogh, *La Moisson* (The Harvest), 1888, oil on canvas, 72.5 x 92 cm. Rijksmuseum Vincent van Gogh, Amsterdam.

110. Van Gogh, *Les Oliviers, ciel orange* (Olive Trees, Orange Sky), 1889, oil on canvas, 74 x 93 cm. Art Museum, Göteborg.

Les Oliviers (Olive Trees), 1889, oil on canvas, 72.5 x 92 cm. Mrs. John Hay Whitney Collection, New York.

111. Van Gogh, *La Nuit étoilée* (Starry Night), 1889, oil on canvas, 73 x 92 cm. The Museum of Modern Art, New York.

La Nuit étoilée (Starry Night), 1888, oil on canvas, 72.5 x 92 cm. Musée d'Orsay, Paris.

112. Van Gogh, *Café-Terrasse de la place du Forum* (The Terrace of the Café on the Forum Square), 1888, oil on canvas, 81 x 65,5 cm. Kröller-Müller Museum, Otterlo.

113. Van Gogh, *Café de nuit* (Café at Night), oil on canvas, 70 x 89 cm. Yale University Art Gallery, Newhaven.

La Salle de danse (The Ballroom), 1888, oil on canvas, 65 x 81 cm. Musée d'Orsay, Paris.

114. Van Gogh, *Le Jardin fleuri* (The Flower Garden, Arles), 1888, oil on canvas, 95 x 73 cm. Private Collection, Zurich.

115. Van Gogh, *Vignoble à Auvers* (Vineyard at Auvers), 1890, oil on canvas, 64 x 80 cm. Saint Louis Art Museum.

La Plaine près d'Auvers (The Plain near Auvers), 1890, oil on canvas, 73.5 x 92 cm. Bayerische Staatsgemäldesammlungen, Munich.

116-117. Van Gogh, *Le Semeur* (The Sower), oil on canvas, 64 x 80.5 cm. Kröller-Müller Museum, Otterlo.

118. Seurat, étude finale pour *Un dimanche après-midi à l'île de la Grande Jatte* (Final Study for a Sunday Afternoon at the Grande Jatte), 1884-1885, oil on canvas, 70.5 x 104.2 cm. The Metropolitan Museum of Art, New York.

119. Seurat, *Un Dimanche après-midi à l'île de la Grande Jatte* (A Sunday Afternoon at the Grande Jatte), (détail), 1884-1885, oil on canvas, 207 x 308 cm. Art Institute, Chicago.

120. Seurat, *La Seine à Courbevoie* (The Seine at Courbevoie, 1885, oil on canvas, 81.4 x 65.2 cm. Private Collection.

121. Seurat, *Coin d'un bassin* (Corner of a Pool at Honfleur), 1886, oil on canvas, 81 x 65 cm. Kröller-Müller Museum, Otterlo. Argenteuil, 1874.

BIBLIOGRAPHIE

Bernard (Bruce), *The Impressionist Revolution*, Londres, 1986. Trad. franç., Paris, 1991.

Callen (Anthea), *Les peintres impressionnistes et leur technique*, Paris, 1991.

Clay (Jean), *Comprendre l'impressionnisme*, Paris, 1989.

Denvir (Bernard), *Chronique de l'impressionnisme. L'Histoire d'un mouvement jour après jour*, Paris, 1993.

Herbert (Robert L.), *Impressionism : Art, Leisure and Parisian Society*, Yale University, 1988, 1991. Trad. franç., Paris, 1988, 1991.

Huyghe (René), *La Relève du réel : impressionnisme, symbolisme*, Paris, 1974.

Levêque (Jean-Jacques), *Les Années impressionnistes*, 1870-1889, Courbevoie, 1990.

Levêque (Jean-Jacques), *L'Impressionnisme dans le monde, 1860-1920*, Paris, 1990.

Leymarie (Jean), *Dessins de la période impressionniste de Manet à Renoir*, Genève, 1969, 1985.

Leymarie (Jean) et Melot (Michel), *Les Gravures des impressionnistes : Manet, Pissarro, Renoir, Cézanne, Sisley (œuvre complet)*, Paris, 1971.

Miquel (Pierre), *Le Paysage français au XIXe siècle : l'école de la nature*, 3 vol., Mantes-la-Jolie, 1975.

Monneret (Sophie), *L'Impressionnisme et son époque : dictionnaire international illustré*, 4 vol., Paris, 1978-1981.

Rewald (John), *The History of Impressionism*, New York, 1946, 1973. Trad. franç., Paris, 1975, 1986.

Rewald (John), *Post-Impressionism from van Gogh to Gauguin*, New York, 1956, 1962. Trad. franç., Paris, 1961, 1987.